HOW TO WRITE EXAM PREPARATION MATERIALS

Roy Norris

TRAINING COURSE FOR ELT WRITERS

How To Write Exam Preparation Materials
By Roy Norris
This edition © 2020 ELT Teacher 2 Writer
www.eltteacher2writer.co.uk

Although every effort has been made to contact copyright holders before publication, this has not always been possible. If notified, ELT Teacher 2 Writer will endeavour to rectify any errors or omissions at the earliest opportunity.

Contents

ABOUT THE AUTHOR		5
AIMS AND INTRODUCTORY TASK		7
1	WRITING EXAM MATERIALS VS GENERAL MATERIALS: SIMILARITIES AND DIFFERENCES	10
2	VOCABULARY AND GRAMMAR	16
3	LISTENING	31
4	READING	47
5	WRITING	59
6	SPEAKING	81
COMMENTARIES ON TASKS		85
GLOSSARY		100

About The Author

I've always loved language and languages and can still remember declensions and conjugations I learnt in my first year of Latin over 40 years ago. Being a bit of an obsessive, I like the fact that there's a system to be mastered, a set of rules and commonly occurring language chunks that create a certain amount of order out of what at first seems like a random and chaotic jumble of words. It's probably no coincidence that I eventually became an ELT materials writer: it's given me the chance to organise language and help make it more accessible to learners. Before that, I'd taught French and German in a secondary school in Yorkshire, England and then spent several years teaching English at International House (IH), both in Madrid, where I live, and Vilnius, where I worked as Director of Studies for a year and a half. It was there in Lithuania, that I first started writing materials for my own classes and those of other teachers.

When I came back to Spain, a number of colleagues encouraged me to try and get something published. I let it be known to as many people as possible that I wanted to write, including editors at the local offices of one or two publishers in Madrid. My big break, though, came at the Madrid TESOL conference in 1999, where I was giving a talk on preparing students for the FCE exam. The late David Riley was present: he had previously been at IH and was now working as a publisher for Macmillan. He passed my name on to Sarah Curtis, the commissioning editor in the exams department, who was looking for someone to write a new FCE course. I wrote a sample unit, which they liked and 18 months later my first course, *Ready for FCE*, was published.

I knew nothing about writing materials for publication at the beginning of those 18 months and had to pick things up as I went along – it was an incredibly steep and stressful learning curve. It's for this reason that I wanted to write this book; to pass on the knowledge that I have acquired over the years, to put down in writing the things I wish I had known when I started out all those years ago. Writing ELT materials is always going to be hard work, but I hope this ebook makes things at least a little easier for you.

I wrote *Ready for FCE* and a couple of other courses on my own, but I've also had the good fortune to work with co-authors Amanda French (New Zealand), and Lynda Edwards (New Forest) on other projects. Equally importantly, I've had the privilege and luxury of working with some excellent editors, in particular Helen Holwill, Amanda Anderson, Rónán McGuinness, Jane Coates and Sarah Forbes – their enthusiasm, dedication, attention to detail and human qualities have been of enormous support. This book is dedicated to them and everyone else I've mentioned above, as well as the many other people who have helped and encouraged me over the years.

Aims And Introductory Task

The basic aims of this module about writing exam preparation materials are to:

1. provide an overview of the similarities and differences between writing exam materials and writing general materials.

2. provide an insight into how exam tasks are constructed for testing students' knowledge and abilities in the four main skill areas as well as vocabulary and grammar.

3. give advice on how to write exam preparation and practice materials, for your class, your school or for publication.

4. offer practical time-saving tips to help make the whole writing process a little smoother and easier for you.

5. encourage you to think critically about exam materials.

NOTE

This module can only offer general advice on how to write and prepare for task types which appear in a number of different examinations. It is important to study past papers of the specific exam for which you are preparing students and keep clear records of how the various tasks are constructed. In this way, you can imitate the exam style more closely and ensure that students have relevant practice. The notes you make in Task 1 (page 8) will be useful in this respect.

Task 1

1. Before you start this book, find one example of each of the following in an exam for which you would like to write practice material:

- a reading text and accompanying questions
- a listening task, including the script
- a multiple-choice cloze or an open cloze test[1]

2. Make notes on the following for each of your three examples:

- the general **subject matter** of the text or script
- the **style** (e.g. *light-hearted*) and **register** (e.g. *informal*) of the text or script
- the **number of words** in the text or script
- the **intervals at which answers appear** in the text or script. E.g. *There are usually 50–60 words separating each answer in the listening script.*
- the **nature of the items tested**. In the case of the listening script and reading text, this might, for example, be opinion, attitude, emotions, detailed facts and/or gist[2] or additionally, in the case of reading, text structure. In the cloze text, are the tested items primarily lexical[3],

---

[1] **open cloze test**
A gap-filling task in which words have been removed from a text. Unlike the **multiple-choice cloze test**, students are given no options to choose from and have to come up with the answers themselves.

[2] **gist**
The gist is the general idea or meaning conveyed by the writer in a reading text or a speaker in a listening script.

[3] **lexical**
Lexical is the adjective from *lexis* and relates to vocabulary.

grammatical or a combination of both? Do the lexical items form part of collocations[4] in the text? Is there a predominance of one particular word class? And so on.
- likely **incorrect answers and the reasons** why students might choose the wrong answer. In the case of the listening and reading tasks, this might be because of the wording in the script or text. A multiple-choice cloze test[5] may have distractors[6] which are similar in meaning to the correct option, but do not fit the sentence grammatically.

Keep these examples, together with your notes, so that you can use them as a point of reference during this module.

---

[4] **collocation**
A collocation is a pair or group of words that commonly occur together e.g. *bitterly disappointed, a wide range of goods, provide an insight into.*

[5] **multiple-choice cloze test**
A gap-filling task in which words have been removed from a text. Students are given a number of options for each gap and they have to decide which of these options best fits the gaps.

[6] **distractor**
Distractors are the incorrect options in a multiple-choice question.

1. Writing Exam Materials vs General Materials: Similarities And Differences

ELT writers need to be able to combine a strong element of creativity with a healthy attention to detail, and writers of exam materials are no exception in this respect. A lack of creativity can lead to dry, dull and uninspiring materials; and a sloppy approach to writing will lead to confusion and unreliable test exercises. Arguably, though, writers of exam materials need to pay *even more* meticulous attention to detail than writers of general materials, particularly if they are following a model established by an external examination board. They need an intimate knowledge of the exercise types in a particular exam in order to be able to imitate them as closely as possible – or at least be aware when they deviate from the model and can justify their reasons for doing so.

Here are some further similarities and differences between the two types of writing. First, the differences:

SOME DIFFERENCES

When writing preparation materials for a specific exam, there is a clearly defined objective to achieve, requiring the provision of practice in a number of fixed task types, each with specific characteristics relating, for example, to length, number of test items, type of text and so on. There may also be a topic syllabus or a set of linguistic aims which have been laid down by an exam board or a school. Some writers might see this as limiting, a constraint which general materials writers do not face. It might also, however, be considered an advantage – the goals are already established and there are no major decisions to make as to which types of task to write or how to construct them.

When writing coursebook materials, with so much focus on exam-style tasks it becomes more of a challenge to ensure that classroom lessons have sufficient flow and student interaction, with plenty of opportunities for speaking. These are essential elements in all coursebooks, of course, but the need to provide so much text-based practice makes this doubly difficult with exam materials. Certainly, exam students should be motivated to learn, as their aim is to pass the examination they are preparing for, but it is important that the materials they use are engaging and help to make the experience an enjoyable one.

Indeed, exam materials often need to achieve more aims than general materials. In addition to providing exam practice and training in exam skills they might also have to build students' language store and improve their general language skills. This can affect the way tasks are designed; a listening script, for example, might need to include previously presented language, provide examples of vocabulary and/or structures to be exploited post-listening, imitate an exam task in terms of style, content and length, and be engaging, with points for post-listening discussion as well. This can be a tall order, and incorporating all of these aspects in a listening exercise requires extremely careful planning.

Exam tasks and therefore exam practice material can be very text-heavy, taking up a large amount of space on the page. For example, an exam reading text with seven multiple-choice questions, each with four options, and each option on its own line, will take up far more space than a non-exam reading task with slashed options. Compare the following:

Exam format

1. How did Charles feel when he read the letter from his aunt?
A distressed at the news of her illness
B disappointed that he could not visit her
C annoyed that she had not written sooner
D sorry that he had not contacted her himself

Alternative non-exam format

1. When Charles read the letter from his aunt, he felt distressed at the news of her illness / disappointed that he could not visit her / annoyed that she had not written sooner / sorry that he had not contacted her himself.

In the case of commercially-produced materials, this can leave little room for visual material and lead to very dense, print-heavy pages with few or no photos or illustrations to brighten them up. For this reason, it is all the more important that text-based exercises do not exceed the word limits established in the specifications for the target exam.

SOME SIMILARITIES

Planning is essential, whatever the nature of the material you are writing – whether it is exam or non-exam material, and whether it is for a specific class, a set of digital materials or a coursebook. For an individual cloze text, for example, the following points may need to be considered before you start writing:

- The length of the text and, if relevant, whether and how it will fit on the page with other materials you have written.

- The subject matter and how it relates to other materials you have written.
- The style and register of the text.
- The number of items to be tested (in the text as a whole and in each sentence).
- The nature of the items to be tested (e.g. vocabulary and/or grammar, word class, words which have been seen recently and/or words encountered some time ago).
- Possible pre- and post-exercise discussion and/or language work.

And before writing a set of materials or a coursebook – both exam and non-exam – there are major decisions to be made regarding the content and layout of each module or unit: how many readings and listenings each unit will have; whether each unit will follow the same progression and start, say, with a speaking activity or whether it can sometimes begin with a reading or listening task; the amount of vocabulary recycling you hope to include; the frequency and distribution of each task type throughout the materials, and so on.

You also need to consider any systems you wish to introduce, and plan where and how often you want to provide relevant teaching slots. This might include sections on word formation (affixation[7]), phrasal verbs, collocations,

---

[7] **affixation**
Affixation is the process of adding material to a word to create a different form of that word (e.g. *tree* → *trees*), a word which is a different part of speech (e.g. *sad* → *sad**ness***) or a word with a different meaning (*happy* → ***un**happy*). The parts shown in bold in the examples are known as *affixes*. Affixes which are added to the end of the base word (e.g. ***-ness***) are called suffixes; those added to the beginning of the base word (e.g. ***un-***) are called prefixes.

paraphrasing[8] and other sub-skills.

As with teaching, it is much easier and safer to write a plan and then, if necessary, deviate from it, than to make up your plan as you go along.

A sense of progression should be built into both exam and non-exam materials which are to be used on a course of study. Non-exam materials intended to take students to a B2 level, for example, will most probably begin at a similar level to where the B1 materials ended and become progressively more challenging. Similarly, materials which prepare students for a B2 level examination over a period of weeks or months will not include tasks at the level of the exam in the early stages of the course. Whilst tasks can certainly imitate those in the exam in terms of format, it makes sense if the level of difficulty of both the language and the questions is *initially* lower than in the actual exam. If relevant, this will also enable writers at the beginning of the course to focus on explaining how the tasks work and suggest appropriate techniques for how to complete them. As the course progresses, this support can be removed and the level of difficulty of the tasks increased.

Finally, if you are writing materials for publication, it is wise to think beyond the publication date of the book and consider, if relevant, its promotion. As well as being a pedagogical tool for helping students pass an exam and/or increase their language skills, a book is also a commercial product which, presumably, you would like to be successful, whether you are paid royalties or not. It therefore needs to be thorough, both teacher- and student-

---

[8] **paraphrase (n/v)**
If you paraphrase what someone has written or said, you express the same meaning using different words. E.g. *She probably won't come* is a paraphrase of *She's unlikely to come*.

friendly, attractive in terms of design and also, one might expect, offer something which other books of the same type do not. This may be something which the publisher has thought out – a grammar supplement, a wealth of supplementary online material, a team of people to mark written work in self-access material – or it may be a technique, exercise type or training in a sub-skill which is useful for exam preparation but which no other coursebook provides. This is where you, the writer, come in. Give the sales team an angle, a unique selling point (USP), which will make it easier for them to sell it and, if relevant, help you to promote it.

2. Vocabulary And Grammar

An important part of exam preparation materials is to provide activities which build students' range of vocabulary and grammatical structures. This is a huge area and beyond the scope of this particular book. For more information, refer to other titles in the ELT Teacher 2 Writer series of books. However, students clearly also need practice in completing the types of tasks they will encounter in the exam. In this section we will focus on how to go about writing two task types which are common to many exams: multiple-choice cloze tests and open cloze tests.

MULTIPLE-CHOICE CLOZE TESTS

Multiple-choice clozes are a common way to test students' knowledge and understanding of vocabulary in context. These consist of a short text with a number of gaps, each representing a missing word or phrase. For each gap students are usually given three or four words or phrases, from which they have to choose the one which fills the gap correctly. Here are some points to bear in mind when writing exercises of this type.

Which words should I gap?
Clearly, you should aim to gap a range of different parts of speech within an exercise, particularly verbs, nouns, adjectives, adverbs and linking words. Note, though, that gapping verbs, as you will see in the task below, often requires students to consider the grammar of vocabulary, in addition to collocation and meaning. For this reason, verbs often feature prominently in this task type.

Note that even at C1 level, the actual words gapped and the distractors in this type of exercise are very often fairly frequent items of vocabulary which students are familiar with, rather than 'difficult' words which students may or may not yet have encountered. The challenge for students comes from choosing the right word to complete a collocation or set phrase, to fit in with the surrounding grammar and/or to express the appropriate meaning for the given context.

It would be unusual, and probably unfair, to gap two words in the same clause, particularly if the answer to one gap is dependent on the answer to the other, as in the following example:

> *We're both busy at work this week so we'll probably find we have to (1) _____ the packing for our weekend trip to London (2) _____ Friday evening.*
>
> *1.*
> *A leave*
> *B put*
> *C do*
> *D make*
>
> *2.*
> *A in*
> *B on*
> *C at*
> *D until*

The key could be either:
1 A, 2 D
or
1 C, 2 B
so this is clearly a situation to be avoided if we don't want to create confusion.

What do I need to bear in mind when writing distractors?

If you are preparing students for a specific external exam,

look at past papers to see which, if any, of the following points apply.

1   The options may all be the same part of speech. They might, for example, all be nouns, rather than a mix of nouns and verbs, and if so, they might all be singular, uncountable or plural. For example:

Unable to find the missing documents ourselves, we decided to employ the _____ of a private detective.
*A **services**   B provisions   C features   D facilities*

2   The options may all be from the same semantic field or perhaps similar in form and/or appearance, as in these examples:

Given the president's _____ record for lying, it is clear that most of his election promises will go unfulfilled.
*A path   B course   C **track**   D lane*

There was a poor _____ for last election – only 32% of the electorate voted.
*A breakout   B handout   C **turnout**   D workout*

Failing that, there may be two distinct pairs of words, as in this example:

The flight leaves at 8.30 in the morning so you'll need to _____ early for the airport.
*A put off   B put away   C **set off**   D set away*

The aim is to avoid any one of the options standing out in any way and giving the appearance of being either clearly right or clearly wrong.

3   In exams for monolingual groups of students, distractors may include false friends, or words commonly misused by the target students.

Task 2

The following multiple-choice cloze test is aimed at students who are finishing a B2-level course. Read the text, together with the gapped words in **bold** below, then write three distractors for each of the ten questions, using the advice in *italics* to help you.

My ukelele

You only had to hear my parents sing to know they were both tone deaf, and as (1) _____ as I was aware, neither had ever so much as touched an instrument in their distinctly non-musical lives. (2) _____ , for reasons they were never quite able to explain satisfactorily to me, they both (3) _____ I should learn to play the ukelele when I was just seven years old. It (4) _____ out to be an inspired move. The sight and sound of the ukelele never failed to (5) _____ a smile, and playing it seemed to earn me instant popularity, which did wonders for my self-confidence.

Mr Stevens would (6) _____ to our house once a week and teach me the chords to traditional tunes, or else songs which were popular at the time. He was a huge bear of a man, who seemed to (7) _____ up the whole room, and gave his own ukelele the appearance of a doll's toy guitar. He can't have been (8) _____ very much by my parents – they had little enough money for themselves – but he set about the task of teaching me with (9) _____ enthusiasm. And for that reason (10) _____ , I couldn't help liking him.

19

1. A   **B far**   C   D
Consider other common phrases with the pattern 'as ... as'.

2. A   B   C   **D However**
Consider either three other contrast linkers, or else a mix (e.g. result, purpose, time, etc.)

3. A   B   **C decided**   D
Transitive verbs make good distractors for intransitive verbs.

4. **A turned**   B   C   D
Consider the overall meaning of the clause or sentence when choosing distractors.

5. **A raise**   B   C   D
In this verb + noun collocation, raise *means elicit, cause, provoke, get, produce. You could consider choosing synonyms for a different meaning of* raise *as your distractors.*

6. A   B   C   **D come**
Consider other verbs of movement which might fit if the preposition were different or not there.

7. A   **B take**   C   D
Consider these verbs as distractors for phrasal verbs: bring, come, do, get, give, make, put, take, turn, and/or consider the meaning of the whole clause as in 4 above.

8. A   B   **C paid**   D
Consider exploiting the fact that the passive can only be used with transitive verbs.

9. A **great**   B   C   D

Finding tempting distractors in the same semantic area as great *is not as easy as it may at first seem; a word which sounds wrong may turn out to be an acceptable collocate of* enthusiasm. *Check your ideas carefully (internet, resource books) before making your final choices.*

10. A   B   C   **D alone**

You might have considered using only, lonely *or* solo, *but the first of these would be correct and the other two are not really tempting. Aim for more challenge here.*

You can read a commentary on this task on page 85.

Further comments
I wrote the above text myself to enable me to display certain features and points to bear in mind when writing distractors. Certainly, you can use authentic texts, but writing your own gives you more control over the level of the language and the items to be tested, enabling you to include vocabulary that students have seen in class or a particular coursebook unit.

The ukelele text is around 200 words long, which is a sensible length for an exercise testing ten items. The gapped words are evenly distributed, with five gaps in each of the two similar-length paragraphs. Six of the ten items tested in the text are verbs, which is a common ratio for this type of task; see my comments above on which words to gap.

Finally, don't be surprised if you need several hours to construct an exercise like this. It can take time and careful research to write a natural-sounding, coherent and cohesive text which contains the items you want to test, together with tempting distractors.

Time-saving tips
Keep copies of rubrics to cut and paste each time you write a specific exercise type. For the multiple-choice cloze, create a template with question numbers and letters for the options. This example is for *B2 First* (formerly known as *Cambridge English: First (FCE)*) exercises:

For questions 1–8, read the text below and decide which answer (A, B, C or D) best fits each gap. There is an example at the beginning (0).

0   A   B   C   D
1   A   B   C   D
2   A   B   C   D
3   A   B   C   D
4   A   B   C   D
5   A   B   C   D
6   A   B   C   D
7   A   B   C   D
8   A   B   C   D

OPEN CLOZE TESTS

Open cloze tests are commonly used to test students' knowledge of grammar, though there may also be a lexico-grammatical[9] focus. Open clozes normally consist of a short

---

[9] **lexico-grammatical**
Lexico-grammatical describes areas of language which involve considerations of both lexis and grammar. The lexical phrase *a great deal of* is followed by an uncountable noun such as *money*, whereas *a large number of* is followed by a plural countable noun such as *coins*. Similarly, *cause* and *result* are two items of lexis with a similar

text with a number of gaps, each of which students have to fill with the correct word (usually one). Unlike multiple-choice cloze tests, there are no sets of words from which students choose the answer; they have to think of each word themselves. Here are some points to bear in mind when writing exercises of this type.

Which words should I gap?
Words with a grammatical focus may be gapped, such as articles, prepositions, pronouns, relative pronouns, possessive adjectives, determiners and auxiliary verbs.

The gapped words may also have a lexico-grammatical focus, such as linkers or words which form part of phrasal verbs or set phrases. Here are some examples:

> *... it rained nearly every day. _____ the weather was bad, we had a wonderful time and would definitely go back there.* [Although/Though]
>
> *The president has _____ in for a great deal of criticism recently over his government's economic record.* [come]
>
> *The event will _____ place on Friday 20th June at 6pm.* [take]

Note that phrases and collocations which include verbs such as *bring, come, do, get, give, make, put, take* and *turn* lend themselves well to gapping in open cloze exercises, particularly when no other answer is possible. Here are

---

meaning but different grammar: *cause* is a transitive verb followed by a direct object (*The earthquake caused widespread destruction*); *result* is followed by the preposition *in* (*The earthquake resulted in widespread destruction*).

some more examples, all of which might be tested at level B2 or above:

*Visit the museum and **take** a step back into the past.*

*The clothes were of no use to her so she decided to get **rid** of them. Some she threw away, some she gave to charity.*

*Waste from the factory will continue to pose a health risk for many years to **come**.*

*To have any chance of passing, you need to **make** much more of an effort.*

Other word combinations which might be targets for gapping include two- or three-word phrases such as *so far, as well as, by the way* and even *such as*. Depending on the support from the surrounding text, any one of the words in these combinations could be gapped, provided that numerous alternative answers would not be possible, as explained in the next point.

Avoid gapping words which allow for multiple keys[10], as in this example:

If you look carefully, you ___ see a shooting star.

---

[10] **multiple keys**
If a question has multiple keys, it means a number of different answers are possible. In the following sentence, for example, the words *While, Whilst, Whereas, Although, Though* can all be used to complete the gap:

_____ *some novelists become very wealthy, most struggle to make a decent living.*

Possible answers include a range of modal verbs such as *might, may, could, can, should, will* as well as a number of frequency adverbs like *often, usually, always*, etc. Two or three possible answers for any one gap may be acceptable, and sometimes even four or five (e.g. a gap which allows for *although, though, while, whilst* or *whereas*) but any more would greatly lower the level of challenge and diminish the value of gapping the word.

It is also usual in many official exams not to have a gap where the sentence makes sense and would be acceptable without completing that gap. This might be true of the above example (*If you look carefully, you see a shooting star*) and is a further reason for not gapping the word before the verb *see*. For the same reason, the word *much* in the following sentence would not be gapped (though the word *more* might be).

> *She was very well informed and clearly knew much more about it than I did.*

It can be useful to include gaps in those structures where students regularly make mistakes, particularly if you are writing for monolingual groups. If, for example, students often say *the same that* instead of *the same as,* then you can test their knowledge of this structure by gapping *as* where it occurs in a text after *the same*.

As with multiple-choice cloze tests, it may be unfair to gap two words in the same clause, and/or in situations where the answer to one gap is dependent on the answer to the other, as in the following example:

> *Although he worked (1) _____ hours than me, he got paid much (2) _____ than I did.*

25

The key could be either:
1 more/longer   2 less
or
1 fewer/shorter   2 more

This situation should be avoided, unless, of course, there is further information in the text which makes only one of these two keys possible. Consider the following:

> *Paul worked mornings, whereas I was there from nine to five. But although he worked (1) _____ hours than me, he got paid much (2) _____ than I did.*

Indeed, the further students have to look beyond the words immediately before or after the gap, the greater the level of challenge, and this can be exploited when writing open cloze tests, particularly for higher levels. Consider the features in a) and b) below, which students should be capable of dealing with at B2 level:

a) Unless students read to the end of the sentence in the following example, they might be tempted to complete the gap with an adverb such as *very, quite, rather* or *fairly,* instead of the correct answer, *so.*

> *We enjoyed the holiday very much, but sometimes it was _____ windy by the seaside that we could hardly walk.*

The patterns '*so* + adjective/adverb + *that*' and '*such* + (adjective +) noun + *that*' lend themselves well to this feature, as do conjunctions such as *if, although, but, whereas, while/whilst, before* or *when,* and the preposition *despite.* Consider this example:

> _____ *we saw Jamie Craven in concert last week, we couldn't believe how short he was.* [When]

And the longer the sentence containing the conjunction, the greater the challenge, as students are required to process more text in order to complete the gap correctly.

> *We saw Jamie Craven in concert last week. _____ he performed on stage for nearly three hours and sang over thirty of his greatest hits, he looked as fresh at the end as he did at the beginning.* [Although/Though]

Gapping the words in bold in the following structures has a similar effect:

*At first/Initially ... **but** later ...*
*We didn't (know) ... but we **did** (know) ...*
*not **only/just** ... but ...   the same ... **as** ...*
*more/less ... **than** ...*

It may be possible to gap different words in these structures, such as *not, same* or *more* in the last three.

b) Students who do not take into account what is written in the first sentence below may be tempted to complete the gap with a determiner such as *Some, Many* or *Most*, rather than the correct answer, *These*.

> *In those early days before train travel, the journey to London used to take all day. _____ days you can get to the capital in less than an hour.*

Pairs of words or phrases in contrasts such as *those days/these days* or *some people/others* work well here, as does *however* when used to contrast the ideas in one sentence to those in the preceding one.

> *The hope of the organisers is that the initiative will encourage people to use their cars less frequently. Unfortunately, _____ , it may be too late for this ...* [however, though]

[Note the inclusion of *Unfortunately* to prevent this or other adverbs fitting the gap.]

Task 3

Underline eight words in the following text which you might gap to create an open cloze for B2-level students. **You may make minor adjustments to the text if you think this is necessary.** There is an example at the beginning (0).

(0) Negative words are usually challenging for students to identify. In this case, they need to read the following sentence(s) to understand that *not* is required here. The word *any* could be added between *accept* and *reservations* if it is felt that students need more support here. You would probably need to accept *never* as an alternative key, even though it sounds a little overstated here.

Dining alone
The growing trend in UK restaurants (0) <u>not</u> to accept reservations has a fortunate side-effect for the lone diner. A no-reservations policy can lead to queues forming outside the more popular restaurants as diners wait for a table to become available. Understandably, perhaps, some are far from happy about having to stand outside a doorway before settling down to a relaxing meal. People in parties of four

or more often have a long wait. However, those who choose or are forced to dine alone usually have no trouble getting a table and are seated almost immediately.

This is obviously good news for solo diners, who now make up a significant percentage of the restaurant-going public in the UK. 'A table for one, please' is now a common request to waiters, and people sitting on their own are no longer made to feel as if they are rather odd. They can hold up their head with confidence instead of trying to avoid unwelcome stares from fellow diners.

Extract from: 'Ready for First 3rd Edition' © R. Norris 2013, Published by Macmillan Publishers Limited. Used by Permission. All Rights Reserved.

You can read a commentary on this task on page 86.

Time-saving tips
Keep a record in a separate document of all previously written open cloze tests and their answer keys, which you can refer to each time you write a new exercise of this type. In this way, you can easily ensure you provide a range of practice and do not test the same words or word classes too often.

INTEREST

When writing cloze texts such as those above you will probably also want to provide some advice on exam technique. Encouraging students to read through the whole text before completing the gaps is an obvious start, and a good reason for writing texts which will at least be of some interest to your target students. The principle is the same as for full-blown reading texts: it will make it easier for you to provide pre-reading discussion activities, as well as gist tasks which require students to give the text an initial read-through. This is particularly important when writing cloze texts and other text-based vocabulary and grammar tasks which are intended for use in the classroom, where any opportunity for speaking and engaging with the material is appreciated. In short, cloze texts can, and sometimes need to, be interesting.

3. Listening

In this section we will look at two task types commonly used in exams to test listening skills: multiple-choice questions and sentence completion.

MULTIPLE-CHOICE QUESTIONS

Whilst multiple-choice questions may sometimes be used to test understanding of factual information in a recording, they often focus on aspects such as opinions, feelings, attitudes, purpose or gist. It is common for questions to begin with words and phrases such as *How does the man feel about ...?* or *What does the woman think of ...?* as well as *Why does the woman ...?* or *According to the man, what ...?*

Task 4

Look at the following short dialogue and multiple-choice question, written for a B1-level listening exam. What do you consider to be the good and bad points about the activity? Comment on the following features:

- choice of topic
- language used
- options A–C
- length

Jane: What was your opinion of the steam tractor rally, Paul?
Paul: It was excellent – really cool. I do not think my mother would have enjoyed it very much – she is not one to go in for that sort of thing. But it is really up my street,

I have to tell you. There were tractors of all shapes and sizes and most of them were constructed in the first quarter of the last century – those are the kinds of tractors I am interested in. My only complaint is that I was worn out by the end of the day. There was so much to see.

What did Paul think of the steam tractor rally?
A He found it tiring.
B His mother did not enjoy herself.
C It was not as good as he thought it would be.

You can read a commentary on this task on page 88.

Here is a possible procedure you might like to adopt when writing your own scripts with multiple-choice questions. Each of the four stages begins with advice on what to do, followed by a box with an example for a listening activity at B2 level. Here, we consider a short 30-second dialogue with one multiple-choice question, but the same procedure could be adopted when writing longer scripts with more questions.

1 Idea
Pick a topic and brainstorm different aspects, feelings, reactions, reasons, etc. which you could focus on in your script.

> *Man and woman talking about a hotel. Focus on woman – one thing she didn't like. Mention three of the following: room, food, swimming pool, proximity to beach, staff.*

2 Plan
Write a plan with the ideas you want to include in the question and the script. Consider the correct answer and the distractors (the incorrect options).

How did the woman feel about the hotel?

Answer:
- ***accommodation*** *was inadequate:* room rather cramped – a little uncomfortable
Distractors:
*- the quality of the **food** was poor:* internet reviews said the restaurant wasn't good and there wasn't much choice, but we ate well
*- the **staff** were unfriendly:* man says the waiters were rude and some of the receptionists too. Woman didn't have that experience.

3 Script
Write the script. Be prepared to develop, alter or abandon the ideas from your plan. Aim for coherence[11], cohesion[12]

---

[11] **coherence**
The ability of a text or piece of dialogue to make sense is called coherence. Language which is coherent is clear, well organised and easy to understand. All the ideas and arguments connect or follow in a natural and logical way. Compare the following:

Coherent: Roger Bannister was the first man to run a mile in under four minutes. This historic event took place in Oxford on May 6th 1954.

Incoherent: Roger Bannister was the first man to run a mile in under four minutes. This is not the kind of thing you'd expect her to do so early in the day.

[12] **cohesion**
Cohesion refers to the grammatical and lexical linking that joins together the different parts of a text to give it meaning. Cohesion can be achieved by using devices such as conjunctions (e.g. *but, although, so*), discourse markers (e.g. *as a result, in addition, however, fortunately*), demonstrative adjectives (*this, that, these, those*) and reference pronouns (e.g. *he, him, this, one*).

Note: In the 'incoherent' Roger Bannister example for **coherence** above, there is apparent *cohesion* (the demonstrative pronoun *This* in the second sentence seems at first to refer back to the event in the first sentence) but the lack of *coherence* makes the sentence incomprehensible.

and natural-sounding speech. Read it several times to ensure you achieve this.

> *M: What did you think of the hotel?*
> *W: Not bad. The <u>room</u> was a bit uncomfortable,* **though**. *The bed took up most of it, so it was a bit cramped,* **to be honest**.
> *M:* **Oh really?** *I don't remember* **that** *being an issue when we stayed there.*
> *W: It didn't ruin it for us,* **though**. *The <u>restaurant</u> more than* **made up for it**. **Funnily enough**, *we'd read some pretty bad reports in the online reviews about lack of variety and tasteless meals, but we ate really well there.*
> *M:* **Yes**, **so did we**. **But we did think** *the <u>waiters</u> were a bit rude sometimes – as if they were doing us a favour by serving us.*
> *W: Oh.* **They** *must have left since you were there, then. Ours were lovely.*

- The word *cramped* may be unknown to some students at this level, but there is enough further support in the woman's turn here to make it clear she feels that the accommodation was inadequate.

- The words in **bold** show the attempt to ensure cohesion and flow and make the script sound as much like a natural dialogue as possible, rather than two monologues with a list of unconnected points.

- The script contains approximately 125 words so the recording time will be around 30–40 seconds.

4 Question
Write the question at the same time as the script. Decide whether you want to use different language for each: for example, the words *food, staff* and *accommodation* are mentioned in options A–C below, but not in the script. You

might, however, decide to include some of this language in the script as well, in order to make the distractors even more tempting to students.

> *You overhear a man and a woman talking about a hotel they have both stayed in. How did the woman feel about the hotel?*
> *A She was unhappy with the quality of the food.*
> *B She found some of the staff rather unfriendly.*
> *C She thought the accommodation was inadequate.*

- The example above has three options, A–C; for more challenge – or because of the specific exam for which you are preparing students – you might want to write a fourth.

- Note that options A–C are all approximately the same length. They also each begin with different language: *she was unhappy about, she found, she thought*. The aim is to avoid situations where one option stands out as being clearly different from the others. For the same reason, where options are of different length, it is common for them to be arranged in order of decreasing or increasing length, as in Task 4 (page 31).

- In the following example, options A and B are opposites and therefore mutually exclusive; that is, they cancel each other out. As a result, this type of situation is usually avoided in multiple-choice exercises.

> *What did Richard say about his holiday?*
> *A He had a lot of fun.*
> *B He did not enjoy himself.*
> *C He wanted it to be longer.*

DISTRACTORS

Distractors are the incorrect options in a multiple-choice question. Read the script in stage 3 (page 34) again, as well as distractors A and B in stage 4. Notice how the script does mention the views expressed in A and B, but that these are the opinions of someone other than the woman: in the first case, online reviews; in the second case, the man. This is a common and useful technique for including distraction[13] in a script.

Here are some further ways of including distraction, particularly at B2 level and below. This is not intended as an exhaustive list and other techniques are certainly possible.

1 Desire, hope, expectation or intention
The following verbs, and others like them, can be included in a script to show what the speaker (or other person) wanted, hoped, expected or intended to do **but did not actually do**.

wanted to, hoped to, expected to, intended to, planned on, thought about, was/were going to, tried to, would like to have, was/were supposed to, etc.

This enables you to create distractors using the object of those desires, hopes, expectations or intentions. Consider the following script and question:

> *The kids were away at camp all weekend, and **we were thinking of painting their room** while they*

---

[13] **distraction**
Distraction, here, is used to refer to language included in a reading text or listening script which might cause students to write or choose an incorrect answer.

weren't here. <u>But</u> we couldn't be bothered in the end and decided to make the most of the lovely weather instead. Of course, John's a real nature lover and **he wanted to spend the whole time in the mountains** *going for long walks, <u>but</u> I managed to persuade him we'd be better off on the coast. We had a great time splashing about in the waves.*

What did the couple do at the weekend?
A They spent time at the seaside.
B They went hiking in the countryside.
C They decorated their children's bedroom.

Note the use of *but* after *we were thinking of* and *he wanted to*; other linking devices denoting contrast, such as *though* or *however*, might also be used in the clause or sentence which explains what actually happened.

2 Different (period of) time
Similarly, the following type of language can be used to contrast, for example, what happened in the past (or what normally happens) with **what actually happens or happened** at the time mentioned in the question.

I used to .... but now ...
At one time .... but nowadays ...
At first ... but then ...
As a child, he/she would ... but in later years ...
Normally ... but this time ...

Script: *We used to rent a house on the outskirts, but there wasn't much to do in the evening, so we moved closer to where the action is.*
Distractor: They live on the edge of a city.

3 Unreal past

Past tenses in structures such as conditionals or after *wish* can be used to create distraction, by converting the 'unreal' into the 'real'. Consider the following extracts from scripts and the corresponding distractors:

Script: *I'd probably stay if the boss said he'd pay me more.*
Distractor: Her manager has offered her a salary increase.

Script: *If you'd done what it says on the label, it wouldn't have shrunk.*
Distractor: He followed the washing instructions.

Script: *I wish we'd brought the map and compass with us.*
Distractor: They were well equipped for the walk.

should/could have can be used in a similar way to *wish*:
We should have brought the map and compass with us.

4 Negatives

Negatives (or near negatives) can be used to state the opposite of the information in the distractor, as in these examples:

Script: *It's **not** as if we're desperate for a new car park here.*
Distractor: She thinks the town needs better parking facilities.

Script: *Watching people dance around on stage in tutus is **hardly** my idea of fun.*
Distractor: He enjoys going to the ballet.

Distractors at higher levels

At levels above B2, the principles behind distractors are the same, but the techniques may be slightly more subtle, as in the following example from a longer script in a C1 exam preparation course.

Script
Interviewer: So how was the transition from life assurance representative to teacher?
Richard: Pretty smooth. I was glad to get out of the selling job, to be honest. It just wasn't me – all that false smiling and constant socialising. It'd been a useful learning experience, though – taught me how to stand up and speak to a group of people, how to get an idea across, and I knew that would be a bonus in the classroom. Plus I was ready for all the preparation and marking at home – I realized it was part and parcel of the job. But the money was a bit of a comedown. I'd been earning a decent basic salary before, plus commission – and those days were over now.

Question
How did Richard feel about his new job as a teacher?
A pleased he would now be earning a regular fixed salary
B disappointed at the amount of extra work the job involved
C concerned he might not have the right personality for the job
D confident he could transfer some of his previously acquired skills

Each of the four options begins with an adjective describing a feeling. A and B are not correct because, although the salary and extra work are mentioned, these are not the feelings he expresses. C applies more to his previous job.

Remember

- A distractor for a particular question does not necessarily have to have equivalent language in the script; the fact that the information it contains is plausible but not stated may be enough. However, if both or all the distractors for the question have no grounding in the script, then this is probably an indication that the question is not challenging enough and the script and/or the distractors should be changed.

- Do not force language into a script for the sake of a distractor, if this is done at the expense of cohesion, coherence, consistency of register or naturalness of language. Again, if this occurs, change the script and/or rethink the distractor.

SENTENCE COMPLETION

Sentence completion is generally used to test students' ability to pick out specific information, usually factual in nature, though also sometimes with a focus on opinion. There are several points to bear in mind when writing this type of listening exercise, as the following task will reveal.

Task 5

Compare the following two versions of the same extract from a listening activity, written for a B1/B2 level. The questions and the listening script in each version are different, but the answer key is the same. Consider the strengths and weaknesses of each version, commenting in particular on the level of challenge they present.

Version A

Listen to a scout leader talking to a group of parents about this year's summer camp in Portugal. Complete the sentences with a word or short phrase.

Summer camp
1 The scouts will be sleeping in _____ during their two-week stay in Sao Jacinto.
2 The scouts are going to travel by _____ to Portugal.
3 Parents will pay _____ for their child to go on the camp.
4 The scout leader tells parents to look at photographs of the _____ on the Internet.

Script (with answers in bold)
Well, as you all know, summer camp this year will be in Aveiro, which is just south of Oporto in Portugal. We'll be spending the fortnight in **log cabins** in the Sao Jacinto Nature reserve, an area known for its beautiful sand dunes. We had originally planned to go by plane and train, but that proved quite expensive, so in order to keep the price down, we've decided to hire a **coach** for the journey, which we'll be able to use for trips during our stay in Portugal as well. It's not the fastest way to travel, of course, but we're convinced it's the best – and cheapest – solution. In fact, this year's camp is quite a lot cheaper than last year's, when we asked you to pay nearly £600 – as I'm sure you'll remember! This year the cost of the whole camp, including travel, is just **£350** per child, which I think you'll agree is a reasonable amount, given that we'll be there for two weeks. To reserve a place on the camp we'd like you to pay a deposit of £150 into the usual account by 22nd March.

The **beach** is just 400 metres away from the camp. It's huge and we'll be spending most of the time there during our stay, playing games and doing other activities. Have a look at photos of it online when you get home and you'll see just how big it is.

Version B

Listen to a scout leader talking to a group of parents about this year's summer camp. Complete the sentences with a word or short phrase.

Summer camp

1 The scouts will be spending the fortnight in _____ .
2 The organisers have decided to hire a _____ for the journey to Portugal.
3 The cost of the whole camp, including travel, is _____ per child.
4 The scout leader tells parents to have a look on the Internet at photos of the nearby _____ .

Script (with answers in bold)

Well, as you all know, summer camp this year will be in Aveiro, which is just south of Oporto in Portugal. We'll be spending the fortnight in **log cabins** in the Sao Jacinto Nature reserve, an area known for its beautiful sand dunes. In order to keep the price down, we've decided to hire a **coach** for the journey. Now, speaking of price, the cost of the whole camp, including travel, is **£350** per child. To reserve a place on the camp we'd like you to pay a deposit of half that amount into the usual account by 22nd March.

When you get home, have a look on the Internet at photos of the nearby **beach**. It's just 400 metres away and we'll be spending most of the time there during our stay, playing games and doing other activities.

You can read a commentary on this task on page 89.

An alternative approach is to structure the task as a note-taking exercise, which can make the whole job of writing questions easier. Here is a note-taking version of the activity in Task 4 above:

> Summer camp
> **Main points**
> *Type of accommodation:* _____
> *Type of transport used for trip:* _____
> *Total cost per child:* _____
> **Activities**
> *Main location for activities:* _____

Time-saving tips

- When writing sentence-completion or note-taking tasks, make a general plan of your listening script and possible items that you could test in your questions. Better to have a plan from which you can deviate than to have no plan at all and get stuck for ideas half way through your writing.

- As with open cloze tests, keep a separate record of answer keys for sentence-completion and/or note-taking tasks. This will make it easy to check that you are not testing the same item in more than one task (or if you do, you do so knowingly).

FURTHER CONSIDERATIONS

Here are some further points to bear in mind when writing exam-style – and in some cases, general – listening activities.

- If you are writing with a specific national or international exam in mind, find out from past papers the maximum and minimum number of words in a script for each particular task type. When writing your own material, aim to keep within these word limits; overlong listenings can cause students to lose concentration. Even 30 words over the usual maximum can have this effect, particularly if students have to listen to the recording twice. For the same reason, you should also check the usual number of words between each answer in the script, and not go too far over – or indeed, under – this average when writing your own scripts.

- As you write your script, conjure up an image of the person who is speaking the words. Ask yourself what sort of personality they have, what they look like and what their voice sounds like. This all helps to create more natural sounding speech. Writing listening scripts is one of the few opportunities you have as an ELT writer to be truly creative, and it can be fun. In your daily life, listen to and make a conscious note of how different people really speak in a variety of different contexts; if you live in an English-speaking country this is easy; if you do not, then listen closely to English speakers on the radio, on TV, in films and on the Internet.

- Read your script out loud to get a feel for how it might sound when recorded. If you can, ask others to listen and point out any unnatural sounding speech. I remember a time when I was recording material of mine with other teachers with a view to piloting it in the classroom. Everything was going fine until one of my colleagues kept bursting into laughter every time she tried to read out the following line: *He was a fellow firefighter but first and foremost a friend.* I had to rewrite the line.

- Since the ability to distinguish feelings, emotions and attitudes is tested in a number of exams, it's a good idea to keep a record, or at least be aware, of equivalent words and expressions which might be built into listening questions and scripts to provide practice in this area. Here are just two examples:

Feeling/emotion
happy
Words and phrases
cheerful, pleased, glad, content, delighted, thrilled, elated, ecstatic, over the moon, (put somebody) in a good mood, on top of the world, make somebody's day, raise somebody's spirits, cheer (somebody) up

Feeling/emotion
angry
Words and phrases
cross, mad, annoyed, (be/get) worked up, furious, irate, livid, seething, indignant, up in arms, lose one's temper, fly off the handle, blow one's top, hit the roof, go berserk, be in a rage, throw a tantrum, shake one's fist, make one's blood boil

A good source for this type of language is the *Longman Language Activator*. The language you use will depend, amongst other things, on the level for which you are writing and the register of the language in your script.

- If you are writing a coursebook, listening scripts – in the same way as reading texts – are an ideal medium for inputting new vocabulary and structures, as well as recycling previously taught language. This obviously needs to be considered *before* you begin writing your script, together with a number of other factors, some of which have already been mentioned. These include: using natural sounding language; providing an appropriate number of clues in the script to guide students to the correct answer; working credible exam-style distraction into your script; providing sufficient and clear examples of the vocabulary and/or structures you intend to focus on in post-listening exercises; writing on a topic which will engage the target students, with points of interest in the script which might lead to post-listening discussion work, and all this, while keeping within the word limits for the particular task type. With so much to consider – and the last two points are not usually considerations in the exam proper – it may not always be possible to respect those word limits.

4. Reading

In this section we will look at two task types commonly used in exams to test reading skills: multiple matching and multiple choice. Before we do, we should consider the types of texts we use to create our reading tasks.

AUTHENTIC TEXTS: PROS AND CONS

When I began writing ELT materials in the 1990s, the internet was still in its infancy. I had a clunky computer with a dial-up modem and a very slow connection, so most of the articles I used came from newspapers and magazines bought locally or sent out to me in Spain at considerable cost. Some I typed verbatim into my manuscript, then adapted to the level I was writing for; others I used as inspiration and wrote my own texts using the relatively scarce information I had at my disposal. Either way, it was fairly laborious work.

Things are so much easier now. The internet has come of age and a wealth of articles are available on any subject you care to choose, and most of these can easily be cut and pasted into your draft document. And if nothing suitable presents itself, then it's a fairly simple matter to gather any relevant facts and write your own article. But which are better – authentic or self-written texts?

Authentic texts are clearly very desirable and mean that much of your work has already been done for you. You may need to reduce the length or tailor the language level to suit your target students, but the facts, one hopes (but should not always assume), have been well researched and the arguments, one also hopes, have been well thought out and presented in a style appropriate to the genre.

However, in the case of ELT materials for publication, permission to use an article will almost certainly be required from the original publisher and/or writer of the text. There is always a danger that this will be refused, either because they simply do not wish you to use it, or because they do not like the changes you have made. The cost of that permission may also be excessive and your publisher may not be happy about paying it. Before you start writing, always have a conversation with your editor about funds available for clearing third-party permissions so you know where you stand.

Using extracts from novels can be problematic for other reasons. It is extremely difficult to find a six- or seven-hundred-word section of a novel which can stand alone, and does not assume previous knowledge of plot or characters mentioned within it. Examination boards are usually free to adapt such material as much as they need to suit their educational purposes; writers of commercially-produced materials are not.

In some cases, then, writing your own texts may be your only alternative. This can take longer – you may need to spend time researching the facts and, particularly in the case of intermediate to advanced material, it requires a certain amount of skill to imitate the conventions and style of the genre in which you are writing – but it does offer much greater flexibility. It means you have far more control over the content and the language level, and you can include, for example, lexis and structures which have appeared in recent lessons or earlier units of a course. What's more, no permissions are required and you retain absolute control over the material. This means you can very easily change, cut or add to the text at the editing stages if this becomes necessary – and it very often does.

Your decision as to whether you will use an authentic text or write your own will depend on a number of factors; these might include the availability of suitable material, the level for which you are writing, whether your work is for publication or not, the permissions budget of your publisher and last but not least, your skill as a writer.

MULTIPLE MATCHING

Multiple-matching tasks usually consist of one text or several shorter texts accompanied by a number of questions. Students – or candidates – are required to find the specific information in the text or texts which matches these questions.

Below are two of the four short texts which make up a multiple-matching reading task about people with nomadic lifestyles. (You will see the remaining two texts in Task 6 (page 53).) The tested sections of each text are highlighted using bold and underlining, and the corresponding questions are shown in the same formatting immediately afterwards. For the actual task, these questions – together with those for the remaining two texts – would be jumbled up and placed before the four texts in the following way:

Which person says the following?
1 I have become more flexible in my work.   _____
2 My lifestyle suits my personality.   _____
3 Travelling makes it easy to get jobs.   _____
4 *etc.*

Read the texts and the corresponding questions, together with the comments below.

A nomadic lifestyle
We hear from four people for whom travel is an important part of their lives.

A Sally
I always wanted to travel and I like being on my own, but I also enjoy towns and cities and spending time with other people. So I live and work my way around the country in a canal boat, stepping in and out of urban life as I choose. I earn my living as a one-woman theatre company, putting on shows for disabled children in the places I visit.

I'm very different from my parents; they still live in the house they bought when they got married and we never travelled very far when I was growing up. **So my old friends from childhood still think it's weird that I never spend more than a week or so in any one place.** *My only worry is that I'll find it hard to settle in the future. I'm a very restless type and living on a boat certainly satisfies that side of my nature.*

Which person says the following? (Sally)
Some people are surprised by my choice of lifestyle.
My lifestyle suits my personality.

B Lucy
I've taught English in nine countries so far, including Spain, New Zealand, Jordan and now, Vietnam. **Being prepared to move around means I never have problems finding work** *and I think it's helped me become a better teacher, too – I've learnt to adapt to different cultures and respond to the specific problems each type of learner has with the language.*

> *The downside is that, although I've met and worked with a lot of different people, it's <u>hard to get to know them really well</u>, because I'm never in one country for more than a couple of years. We can, and do, keep in touch online, but that becomes fairly superficial after a while and <u>I often lose contact with people</u>.*

Extracts from: 'Ready for First 3rd Edition' © R. Norris 2013, Published by Macmillan Publishers Limited. Used by Permission. All Rights Reserved.

Which person says the following? (Lucy)
Travelling makes it easy to get jobs.
<u>*I have become more flexible in my work.*</u>
<u>*It is difficult to form and maintain close friendships.*</u>

Comments

1. Authentic articles such as these, made up of a number of shorter texts on the same theme, do exist, particularly in magazines and Sunday newspaper supplements, but the level of English is often very advanced and they may require a great deal of adapting to make them suitable for intermediate levels. For this reason, it is often much easier to write multiple-matching texts yourself. The text above on nomadic lifestyles was inspired by a number of separate articles I found on this theme; I took the basic idea and made the rest up.

2. A close comparison of each question with the corresponding part of the relevant text shows that paraphrasing and summarising play an important part when a task such as this is constructed. Compare, for example, *Being prepared to move around means I never have problems finding work* with *Travelling makes it easy to get jobs.*

3   Since the texts are all on the same theme, there is likely to be an element of distraction already built into the task. For example, some students might be tempted to match the question *It is difficult to maintain and form close friendships* with the line of Sally's text where she says: *So my old friends from childhood still thinks it's weird that I never spend more than a week or so in any one place.* If you are writing the text yourself, you can exploit this feature to its full potential.

Note, also, that the first paragraph of Sally's text is untested. However, the content of this paragraph might cause weaker students to be tempted by two of the questions which relate to Lucy: *I have become more flexible in my work* and, to a lesser extent perhaps, *Travelling makes it easy to get jobs.*

4   It is possible to write questions which match up with two separate parts of the same text. This is the case with the question *It is difficult to form and maintain close friendships,* which relates to two parts of the second paragraph of Lucy's text.

Time-saving tips

- When writing multiple-matching reading tasks, it is useful to build up the questions in the way shown above, and then save this first draft. You may have to come back to this version to make cuts, additions and/or other alterations at a later stage.

- The grouping of the differently formatted questions after each individual text makes it easy to see how you initially constructed the task; it may be obvious to you when you are writing the task, but it won't seem so clear a few weeks, or even days, afterwards. Another way to do this is to use different colours for the questions and matching text. In your second version of the document, you will need to mix up the questions and place them all together before the four texts.

- Having differently formatted/coloured sentences makes it easier to check that you have an evenly spread key, e.g. 1 B 2 A 3 D 4 B 5 C 6 A, etc., rather than 1 B 2 A 3 A 4 B 5 A 6 C, etc. Additionally, you could write your key *before* you mix up the questions to help achieve the same objective.

Task 6

Here are the remaining two texts for the multiple-matching reading on nomadic lifestyles.

For the text on Phillip, write two questions, one for each of the two underlined sections.

For the text on Dougie, underline two or three testable sections and write a question for each of them.

The questions should be in the same style as those for the texts on Sally and Lucy above.

C Phillip
As the financial director of a multinational company based in France, I spend my life travelling and I'm rarely in one place for more than six months. Home is England at the moment, but last month it was Milan and before that, Atlanta. I live in hotels or rent for short periods, so the sensation is one of being on permanent holiday.

Living nomadically has shaped my attitude to possessions; I do my best to keep them to the bare minimum and I don't get attached to things. If I have to buy something for a house, like furniture or curtains, I don't mind leaving it behind when I move on. I'm not sure know how long I'll be able to go on with this lifestyle; I've spent the last 12 years focusing on my career and I'd quite like to settle down soon.

D Dougie

I come from a long line of travelling showmen, and for most of the year we tour the country from fairground to fairground. It's been in my family's blood for nearly two centuries. There was someone on my father's side who used to train bears, and another relative who lost a finger working as the assistant to a knife-thrower.

I live in a caravan, with my wife, Janie, and the two kids, and because conditions are a bit cramped, we get on each other's nerves quite a lot. Everyone works really hard; we have to set up all our heavy equipment – usually in the middle of the night – then we're on our feet for hours on end every day for the duration of the fair. And after about a week or so we take it all down again, and move on to the next place. It's a tough life, but I don't see myself doing anything else – there's nothing else I'd rather do.

Extract from: 'Ready for First 3rd Edition' © R. Norris 2013, Published by Macmillan Publishers Limited. Used by Permission. All Rights Reserved.

You can read a commentary on this task on page 91.

MULTIPLE CHOICE

As with multiple-choice *listening* tasks (page 31), the questions you devise may deal with a variety of features, including factual information, opinions, feelings, attitudes, purpose and gist. In addition, you will need to write plausible distractors, that is, incorrect options which are sufficiently tempting for students to choose them as their answer. These are generally based on language and ideas in the reading text, though you may find that this is not always possible, or indeed, necessary.

Also in common with multiple-choice listening tasks is the tendency to avoid situations where one of the four options stands out as being clearly different from the others, either because of the language used, or because it is of a very different length. Mutually exclusive options, those with opposite meanings which cancel each other out (e.g. 'How did the writer feel about the news?' A She was happy. B She was sad.), are similarly avoided. As mentioned previously, it is important to look carefully at examples of the exam for which you are writing material, and gather as much information as possible on how exactly the questions are constructed.

Below are the first two multiple-choice questions from a text about a firm of private detectives. Read the questions and notice in each case how the four options (A–D) are related to ideas and language contained in the text. The key and the relevant part of the text are shown with a single underline; the distractors are shown using the same formatting as the ideas in the text upon which they are based.

> *Private investigators investigated*
> *David Lee investigates the world of the private*
> *eye – and uncovers some surprising truths.*

When I walk into the offices of Wright & Wrong Ltd, a predominantly female firm of private investigators, I am a little disappointed. My only previous contact with private detective agencies has been through black and white films from the golden age of Hollywood. So I am half expecting to see a small, dark, smoke-filled room, a single desk with an empty in-tray and a long, scruffy raincoat hanging from a hat stand.

<u>Clearly, my romantic image of the profession needs updating.</u> Wright & Wrong Ltd's offices are light and spacious *and there are no ashtrays in sight on any of the dozen or so desks. These are <u>tidy and free of paper, but concentrated faces at large computer screens</u>* give the place a busy feel.

1 What does the writer discover on his visit to the offices of Wright & Wrong Ltd?
A <u>The firm is not as dynamic as he had been told.</u>
B The offices have recently been modernized.
C **All the private detectives in the firm are women.**
D <u>He has an old-fashioned idea of private detectives.</u>

Jenny Wright, founder of the agency, is not surprised at my error, and <u>with a note of irritation in her voice, points to further misconceptions.</u> 'Cinema and television are <u>mostly to blame for our reputation.</u> Contrary to popular belief, **we always work very strictly within the law** – there's no <u>violence</u>, no break-ins, and certainly no guns. The laws relating to our activities are very tight, and if we don't stick to them* there's a very real danger that the evidence we obtain will not be accepted in court.'

2 Jenny Wright is annoyed by
A *the strict laws controlling private detectives.*
B the inflexibility of the law courts.
C *the way her profession is represented in films.*
D *the violence used by other detective agencies.*

Extract from: 'Ready for First 3rd Edition' © R. Norris 2013, Published by Macmillan Publishers Limited. Used by Permission. All Rights Reserved.

Task 7

Here are two further extracts from the text above on private detectives, together with the relevant questions. Write the four options (one correct answer and three distractors) for each of the questions.

Most of Jenny's clients are wealthy. The hourly rate is anything between £50 and £80, so the cost of a single case will often run into thousands of pounds. Even with hi-tech equipment, such as long-range listening devices, a surveillance campaign can last several days. 'The technology is freely available and most of what we do could be done by the clients,' explains Jenny, 'but they're reluctant to get involved. Finding out the truth is often just too painful to do on your own.'

3 What do we learn about Jenny's clients?
Advice: *wealthy* is too easy a word to test at B2 level; better to target what Jenny says at the end of the paragraph.

I ask Jenny, a former night club owner, how she came to be a private detective. Her face turns red, she gives a slight grin and drops her voice to a whisper so as not to be

57

overheard by her staff. 'I used to read a lot of crime novels during the daytime,' she confides, 'and I started to think "I could do that". I went on a training course and realized I was in the wrong job.' I am about to ask her whether she ever wears a long, scruffy raincoat, when her mobile phone rings and she is called away on business.

4 How does Jenny feel about telling her story in the last paragraph?
Advice: the options could all be one-word adjectives, each expressing a plausible feeling.

Extract from: 'Ready for First 3rd Edition' © R. Norris 2013, Published by Macmillan Publishers Limited. Used by Permission. All Rights Reserved.

You can read a commentary on this task on page 92.

5. Writing

An actual writing task may take up very little space on the page, but as this section shows, there are many factors to be borne in mind when setting the task and preparing students to write their answers.

SETTING A WRITING TASK

When setting a writing question, be sure to consider whether *all* of your target students will be able to answer it. This may seem obvious, but it is, unfortunately, sometimes overlooked. Ask yourself whether students will have the necessary knowledge, ideas and language to enable them to write a full answer. Certainly, help can be given with ideas and language (see **Ideas and language** below), but if even just a few of your target students have little or no schematic knowledge[14] of a topic, or else the question itself does not allow for a great deal of development (i.e. 'there's not much you can say about it'), then a replacement question or an alternative is needed.

---

[14] **schematic knowledge**
Schematic knowledge refers to what we know about the world and the way it works. For example, if we know and can visualise what happens in a football match – if we have a well-developed schema for football – we will be able to make sense of the following statement: *He was substituted after he got the yellow card; they couldn't afford to lose him for the next match.* If we don't have that particular schematic knowledge, (if we don't know that players can be substituted during a match, what yellow cards are, or that two yellow cards mean a player is sent off and automatically misses the next match) we might struggle to understand the sentence.

Task 8

For each writing task, 1–5, what assumptions have been made about the students who have been asked to write an answer? Are there any potential problems for students? Consider, for example, the students' language level, age, knowledge, experience, possible interests and so on.

Example
Write an essay answering the following question, giving reasons for your views: *Should politicians be paid higher salaries?*

Students will need an awareness of, and interest in, what politicians do, and a general idea of how much they are paid in order to be able to answer this. A certain level of maturity of thought has also been assumed, as this will be required to answer this question successfully, probably at a B2 level or above. Younger students – and some older students – *might* lack one or more of the features just described.

1. Here is part of an email you receive from your English friend. Write a reply to your friend.
We aren't sure where to go for our beach holiday this year and we need some help to decide. Can you recommend a couple of decent places you know? What do you think we'd like about them?

2. Write an essay on the following question: *Is the use of technology in sport a good or a bad thing?*

3. Write a report for the local council on public transport services where you live. Describe what services are available and suggest ways in which they can be improved.

4. Write a story beginning with the following sentence: *She handed in her notice and breathed a sigh of relief.*

5. Your company's in-house magazine is running a series of articles on jobs in management within the company. You have been asked to write an article on your own management position, explaining your role, describing the challenges of the job and the qualities required to meet those challenges.

You can read a commentary on this task on page 93.

IDEAS AND LANGUAGE

When answering exam-style writing questions, students usually need, or at least appreciate, some kind of help when deciding which ideas to incorporate and which language to use in their answers.

When setting a writing task, note down ideas and language which students could include in their answer (or which *you* could include in your model). And if you have problems coming up with ideas, then you probably need to rethink the question.

Consider the question in the example in Task 8 above:

Write an essay answering the following question, giving reasons for your views:
Should politicians be paid higher salaries?

Here are some ideas and language which could be included in an answer:

Ideas

Yes, they should.
They do an important job, have a great deal of responsibility.
If they are not paid enough, they might look for jobs in the private sector.
They are currently paid very little (in my country).

No, they shouldn't.
They are civil servants, paid with public money.
They get money from other jobs.
They are already paid enough (in my country).

Language

Language related to earning money
e.g. *receive a good income, source(s) of income, annual/average earnings, earn more/a great deal of (money), make good/a lot of money, deserve more (money), reward, overpaid/underpaid/highly paid/poorly paid*

Structures
Conditionals: e.g. *if they were paid more ...*
Passives: e.g. *they **are paid** too much already; they deserve **to be paid** more*
Clauses of reason and result: *because, as a result of, owing to, so that, in order to/that*

Task 9

Look again at questions 1–5 from Task 8 (page 60). Select two of the questions and for each one make two lists; one of ideas and another of language that students could use in their answers, as in the example above.

You can read a commentary on this task on page 94.

Providing help with ideas and language

The next stage is to decide how you will present the ideas and language when preparing students to write the task. Here are some ways in which you can do this.

Ideas

a) You could simply ask students to brainstorm ideas and then select the best ones for inclusion in their answers. Depending on the topic area, you could provide general categories under which to make notes. If, for example, students are asked to make a proposal for a school magazine, you might include the following: Articles, Interviews, Reviews, Competitions, Regular columns.

For question 3 in Task 8 (page 60), the brainstorming exercise could take the form of a speaking activity, such as the following:

> *How good are the public transport services in your area? Discuss the following with your partner:*
> *- frequency of services*
> *- number of routes*
> *- comfort*
> *- parking facilities at stations*
> *- facilities for the disabled*
> *- other*

b) Another way is to provide a number of short quotes, opinions which people have supposedly expressed on the topic in the writing task. This is a useful way of giving ideas without spoon-feeding students, and if the opinions are in a different register to that required by the task, students cannot simply copy the language used either. Here are some sample quotes for question 2 in Task 8 (page 60), with a possible task:

Read the following comments and decide whether the speaker feels that technology in sport is a good or a bad thing.

1 I preferred it when we didn't have this goal-line technology – it was far more exciting.
2 Cycling is so much safer now – helmet design has come a long way since the old days.
3 Tennis players don't complain as much as they used to. It's really taken the pressure off the line judges.
4 Who won the race? Was it the swimmer or the swim suit?
5 I might have done better if I'd been able to afford one of those new bikes.
6 It's thrilling to see so many records being broken in the track events. I think the new surface has something to do with it.

c) If you are writing a coursebook, or writing exam material for students you are teaching, then the ideas for the writing section could be input via reading texts, listening scripts and other text-based exercises. For example, a writing question on environmental issues could be preceded by texts and scripts dealing with different aspects of the environment, which might be relevant to the writing task.

d) Language exercises, such as the one in b of **Language** below, can be designed in such a way that they also introduce ideas relating to content and which students can develop in their answers.

e) Students can be given a plan for the writing task containing a brief summary of possible content. See **Planning and Organisation** in Activities With A Model Answer (page 69).

Language

As in a) of **Ideas** above, you could simply ask students to draw on their existing knowledge and brainstorm vocabulary and structures which might be relevant to the task. If, however, your aim is to extend students' range, then you could input new language using one of the following strategies:

a) Simply give students a list of language they could use.

b) Provide an exercise for them to complete. Having to work with the language in this way *might* increase the chance of students actually using it themselves. The following example is just one way of many possible ways of inputting language for question 1 in Task 8 (page 60).

> *Complete each gap with one of these words:*
> *bustling   clean   quiet   range   resort*
> *sand   water   waves*
>
> *1 We stayed in a popular **seaside** _____ .*
> *2 The beaches were all **spotlessly** _____ .*
> *3 We swam each day in **crystal-clear** _____ .*
> *4 We went for long walks on the **soft** _____ .*
> *5 Our children played in the **gentle** _____ .*
> *6 The town itself was very **lively** and _____ .*
> *7 It's not for those who enjoy **peace and** _____ .*
> *8 It offers visitors **a wide** _____ of possibilities.*
>
> *Key*
> *1 resort   2 clean   3 water   4 sand*
> *5 waves   6 bustling   7 quiet   8 range*

c) Include useful language in a model answer (see Activities With A Model Answer, page 68).

Using a model

One particularly effective way of preparing students for an exam writing task is to provide them with a model answer, demonstrating the structure, register, type of language and other techniques they would be expected to use. The model needs to be such that students cannot simply copy large sections of it when writing their own answers (though in the case of some writing task types such as letters of application, they can be encouraged to borrow a number of formulaic chunks of language). With this in mind, the following procedures might be considered:

1   Provide a writing question and model answer. After analysis of the model, students write an answer to a different question, which could be structured in a similar way to the first one.

    Example

    Writing task which would be accompanied by a model answer
    Write an article answering the following question:
    How different would your life be without a mobile phone?

    Writing task for which students would write an answer
    Write an article answering the following question:
    How different would your life be without a car?

    In the above example, students might be encouraged to organize their answer in the same way as the model, employ similar techniques and probably also use some of the same grammatical structures (e.g. conditionals and modal verbs) but the subject matter, ideas and most, if not all, of the lexical content would clearly be very different.

2   Set a writing question which allows for numerous possible answers. The model offers one of these possibilities; students write their own answer to the same question on a different topic.

Example

Write a story ending with the following sentence:
I had never been so surprised in all my life.

3   The writing question includes a number of options, one of which is addressed in the model answer. Students write their own answer to the question, addressing one of the other options.

Examples

a) Write a review for an online website of something you have bought recently. It could be an item of clothing, a smartphone, a car ... anything you like. Describe the good and bad points of your purchase and say whether you would recommend it or not.

b) The school where you study English is recruiting new staff. The jobs available are: library assistant, receptionist, bar staff, events organiser.
Write a letter of application for one of the jobs, explaining why you think you would be suitable.

4   Rather than a model, you provide a badly written answer to the question. After examining why the answer is bad, students write their own, improved answer to the same question.

How good should the model be?

It is likely you will want your model to represent the best type of answer to the writing task and include all the elements that students could incorporate into their own answers. You might also, for example, want to use the model to input new language, which will enable students to perform at a higher level than they are currently capable of. At the same time, you do not want to put students off by presenting them with an answer of a level and quality that they feel they would never be able to produce themselves.

My own feeling is that a model can be used to help students *extend* their capabilities rather than merely reflect what they can already do, and as such should be written at as high a level as might be considered reasonable. As long as the analysis of the model draws attention to aspects of new language and cohesion, for example, (see Activities With A Model Answer below), there is less danger of discouraging students and more chance of getting the best out of them. Your experience and knowledge of the target students' level will be the best tools for helping you decide how much you can expect from students and how good your model can be.

Activities with a model answer

Your model could focus on one or more of a number of features. Here are some ideas for:

1 Planning and organisation
2 Cohesive devices
3 Range of language
4 Register
5 Accuracy
6 All features

1 Planning and organisation
Planning of written answers is essential to ensure clear organisation of ideas. This, in turn, will enable students to use a variety of cohesive devices and a range of vocabulary and structures. It will also help them to answer the question correctly and completely.

The following activities focus on the importance of planning, but also provide an initial gist task – a reason for students to read the model answer before going on to do more detailed analysis, as suggested in sections 2–5 below.

The plans you write need only be in note form, as in this example for the following essay title:

> *Technology has had a positive influence on our lives today. Do you agree?*
>
> ***Essay plan***
> <u>Introduction</u>
> *majority view is positive but not my opinion*
>
> <u>Paragraph 2</u>
> *1 Tablets, laptops in schools – students don't concentrate*
> *2 Mobile phones – obsessive behaviour – an addiction. Also cause car accidents.*

Paragraph 3
3 Causes unemployment, e.g. internet shopping – small shops close. Automatic checkouts – fewer cashiers.

Conclusion
restate opinion

Possible activities

a) Give two (or even three) possible plans for a question. Students read the model answer and identify which plan the model follows.

b) Give just one plan and in the model answer include, for example, an additional point, an omission or a different opinion. Students read the model and identify the difference(s).

c) Ask students to effectively create the plan for the model answer by asking them to identify the purpose of each paragraph. You will probably need to provide an example to ensure students know what is meant here by 'purpose'.

Example

What is the purpose of each paragraph in the following model answer? The first one has been done for you.
Paragraph 1: Thank Paul for his letter. Accept his offer to go and stay.

An alternative would be to summarise the purpose of each paragraph, but put these summaries in the wrong order. Students read the model answer and match each summary to its paragraph.

2 Cohesive devices

Good writing answers include a variety of linking devices. These include linking words and phrases such as conjunctions (e.g. *but, although, so*) and discourse markers (e.g. *as a result, in addition, however, fortunately*). Depending on the level, you might also wish to focus on other aspects of cohesion such as demonstrative adjectives (*this, that, these, those*), reference pronouns (e.g. *he, him, this, one*), possessive adjectives (e.g. *my, his, your*), adverbs of place and time (e.g. *here, there, then*) or substitution and ellipsis (e.g. *His first film was excellent; this one is not.*).

Possible activities

a) Ask students to underline linking words and phrases in the model answer. You will need to have previously made clear to students what is meant by 'linking words and phrases' and you should give one or two examples after your rubric.

b) Gap some of the cohesive devices in the model and put them in a box. Ask students to complete the gaps with the words given. Aim to ensure that there is only one possible answer for each gap.

Example
(Extract from a model article with answers shown.)

> *Complete each gap in the model answer with one of these words:*
> *as   but   however   so   whilst   here   then*
> *this   these   it*
>
> *So (8) whilst it may not be the best job in the world, being a cleaner can't be as bad as many people imagine (9) it is. With all (10) these advantages, I think I'd quite like to have a go.*

c) Ask students to replace the discourse markers in a model answer with alternatives which you provide. To make the task easier, you could underline the discourse markers in the model.

Example
(Extract from a model essay)

> *Replace each of the underlined words or phrases in the model answer with one of these words or phrases which has a similar meaning or function.*
> as a result   furthermore   to begin with
> regrettably   in general   in conclusion
> finally   in fact   however   for instance
>
> *<u>On the other hand</u>, there are a number of disadvantages. <u>Firstly</u>, sedentary jobs involving long periods in front of a computer are known to be a major cause of heart disease. <u>In addition</u>, too much time spent looking at a computer screen can be damaging for a person's eyesight. <u>Unfortunately</u>, many young people nowadays ...*

d) Jumble the order of sentences or paragraphs in a model answer and ask students to reorder them correctly. To do this successfully, they will need to consider both cohesion and coherence.

3 Range of language
Model answers are a useful vehicle for demonstrating the importance of using a wide range of vocabulary and grammatical structures, raising awareness of paraphrasing and also helping students avoid repetition (though, of course, repetition can be used to good effect as a cohesive device).

For the following activities – as with all of the activities in this section – you need to plan carefully the language you wish to include in your model and how you intend to exploit it.

a) Create a multiple-choice activity in which two (or more) of the options are correct. As the example below shows, this technique can also be used for cohesive devices.

Example
(Extract from a model report with answers shown)

> *Cross out **one** word or phrase which does not fit in the sentence for reasons of either meaning, grammar or register.*
>
> *The (1)* aim/purpose/~~reason~~ *of this report is to (2)* consider/~~look~~/suggest *ways to attract more customers to the bookshop.*
>
> *(3)* Firstly/To begin with/~~At first~~, *a few improvements to the area at the front of the shop would help to create the right impression (4)* as soon as/~~during~~/when *customers walk in. It would be a good idea to have a central display with (5)* a number of/~~loads of~~/several *books on offer at discount prices ...*

b) Ask students to replace the underlined items of language in a model answer with alternatives which you provide. This is the same exercise type as in c of 2 Cohesive devices (page 72).

Example
(extract from a model letter)

> Replace each of the underlined phrases with one of these phrases with a similar meaning or function:
>
> that reminds me   I'm really looking forward to seeing   let me know   go on a trip to   aren't fond of   a wide variety of
>
> There are lots of different things to do in the area and (1) <u>lots of different</u> places to see. We could visit some of the local villages and also (2) <u>visit</u> the capital while you're here. Write and tell me if you can come or not and (3) <u>tell me</u> when the best time for you would be. I can't wait to hear from you and (4) <u>I can't wait to see</u> your new boyfriend.
> (5) <u>By the way</u>, is there any food he doesn't particularly like eating. I remember you (6) <u>don't like</u> eating fish – how about Dan?

c) Students complete a table with words and/or phrases from the model.

Example
(rubric and key relating to model essay)

> Write expressions from the model answer under the correct headings below. The first one has been done for you.
>
> **Expressing your own opinion**
> In my opinion
> I personally feel
>
> **Saying what others think**
> many people believe that
> many consider these to be
> it is widely felt that

d) Students search the model for alternative ways of saying the same thing, structures for expressing a particular function or vocabulary related to a particular topic. The following examples show a range of rubric types with possible keys:

Find words in the model answer which are used to avoid repeating the words effect *and* cause.
Key
effect (noun): influence, impact, outcome
cause (verb): lead to, produce, are responsible for, resulting in

Find examples in the model answer of structures for making recommendations and giving advice:
e.g. I'd recommend (eating)
Key
I'd recommend (taking), One idea is (to buy), Make sure you (see), It might be worth (going), Don't forget (to take)

Underline words and phrases in the model which describe price.
Key
not cheap, reasonably priced, no charge, affordable, inexpensive, low-cost

Underline words and phrases used in the model to talk about the sea and the beach.
Key
crystal-clear water, soft sand, gentle waves, spotlessly clean, perfect sunbathing spot

Underline phrases in the model that might be useful when you write your own application letters.

Key
I am writing to apply for, I have a good knowledge of, I have a great deal of experience in, I have a (patient) and (friendly) nature, I would love to have the opportunity to

4 Register
Inappropriate register can have a negative effect on a target reader and an awareness at least of the difference between formal and informal register generally features in writing assessment criteria for exams from level B2, if not before.

a) Incorporate a two-item multiple-choice exercise into the model answer. Students choose the item which is more appropriate, in terms of register, to the task type and target reader.

Example
(extract from a model letter)

> *Underline the more formal alternatives in this letter.*
>
> *(1)* Dear/Hi *Ms Redman*
> *(2)* Just thought I'd let you know/I am writing to inform you *that I shall be unable to attend the seminar on June 20th (3)* because I'm going somewhere else/owing to a prior engagement. *I would be (4)* extremely/ever so *grateful if you could (5)* forward/let me have *copies of any handouts provided by the speaker.*

b) Include a number of words and phrases in the model which are not consistent in terms of register with the rest of the answer. Underline them and ask students to replace them with more appropriate items which either you provide or, for more challenge, they have to come up with themselves.

Example
(extract from a model report)

> *Replace the underlined phrases in the model with these more formal alternatives:*
> as forecast   the current trend continues
> slightly   clear from the evidence
> there was a significant rise
>
> *Prices decreased <u>a little bit</u> at the beginning of the year, but <u>they went up by a massive amount</u> in the second quarter, <u>just as everyone said they would</u>. It is <u>pretty obvious</u> that spending will fall considerably if <u>things go on like this</u> much longer.*

c) Students look for examples in the model of aspects of informal language.

Example with key

> *Find examples in the model answer of the following features of informal language:*
> *Phrasal verbs:* find out, get on with, give up, take on
> *Contractions:* wouldn't, there's, don't, it's, they're
> *Informal linking words and phrases:* And, But, So, On top of all that, Anyway
> *Informal punctuation:* They can do it – I think I would, too.
> It's excellent!

5 Accuracy

Errors can be included in model answers for students to find and correct. Generally speaking, in order to avoid confusion (usually involving students trying to correct language which is already correct), it is advisable:

- to point out in the rubric the type(s) of mistakes students should focus on.

- to limit the number of different types of mistakes you include (e.g. spelling and punctuation, or verb forms, participle adjectives and dependent prepositions), though this may depend on the level of your students, areas of recent study and/or the stage they have reached in their exam preparation.

- not to include an excessive number of mistakes. Ten mistakes in a model of 200 words is a sensible maximum.

- to include only mistakes which are typically made by students at the target level.

Here are two examples of rubrics together with possible keys for a B2 level.

Example 1

Key
Incorrect spelling	*Correct spelling*
1 freinds	friends
2 usualy	usually
3 dissapointed	disappointed
4 acomodation	accommodation
5 posible	possible
6 definately	definitely
7 neccesary	necessary
8 intrested	interested

Example 2

There are eight grammatical mistakes in the model answer. Correct the mistakes, paying particular attention to the following areas of grammar:
comparative structures
word order
gerunds and infinitives

Key
1 feels ~~more~~ hotter
2 is easier ~~that~~ **than** people think
3 ~~always it is~~ **it is always** better
4 you may not feel like ~~to go~~ **going**
5 ~~they never have~~ **they have never** been
6 only if you need ~~doing~~ **to do** it
7 and you want **to** do it
8 not quite as ~~older~~ **old** as they look

6 All features

Later on in a course, when all the above features have been dealt with in some way, a model can be followed by a simple checklist, such as the one below, covering most or all of these areas. Models can, of course, be good in all areas, though it is more challenging, more realistic and possibly more useful, if the model has a mixture of good and bad elements. In this case, it should perhaps be called a sample answer rather than a model.

Read the sample answer and discuss the following questions about it. Give examples to support your views.

Content *Has the question been answered completely and correctly?*
Register *Has the answer been written in a*

register appropriate to the task and the target reader?
Range *Has the writer used a range of appropriate vocabulary and structures?*
Cohesion *Has the writer used a variety of linking words?*
Organisation *How well are the ideas organized into paragraphs?*
Accuracy *Have all words been spelled correctly? Is the grammar accurate?*

Alternatively, you could provide two models and ask students to compare them, using the same criteria as above.

Time-saving tips

When planning writing preparation sections, list all those features you want to highlight and then tick each one off as you incorporate it into your section. In addition, list any relevant vocabulary items and grammatical structures (particularly those from the current or previous units if you are writing a coursebook) and try to include some in your model answer, as long as they are appropriate and can be used naturally.

6. Speaking

Clearly, speaking is a very different skill to writing, but as with writing, students need help with ideas and language when performing speaking tasks. Much of what we saw in Providing Help With Ideas And Language (page 63) is also relevant here, so in this section we will focus our attention instead on one or two factors which need to be taken into consideration when writing picture-based tasks and discussion questions.

Picture-based tasks

Some of the tasks in the speaking paper of the exam for which you are writing may be built around photographs. When sourcing these for your own tasks, you could use one of the following online photo libraries which offer free use of their images under Creative Commons licences. This list is by no means exhaustive.

Unsplash – *unsplash.com*
Pixabay – *pixaby.com*
Pexels – *pexels.com*
Nappy – *nappy.co*

If your material is intended for publication, your publisher may have its own library, containing photographs and illustrations which they have permission to use in multiple publications. Note also that publishers may have arrangements with certain libraries for preferential rates ask your editor before you start writing. If you decide, for whatever reason, not to use the photographs in the publisher's own library, there are a number of factors to be borne in mind when selecting alternatives from sites such as those above, as the following task will show.

How To Write Exam Preparation Materials

Task 10

Imagine you are writing material which is intended for publication and which will be sold in a number of different countries worldwide. You have briefed for the following photographs for use in your speaking tasks. What problems, if any, might there be in using each of these photographs in your material?

1. A school canteen with some 80 or more uniformed children eating their lunch.

2. A farmer feeding his pigs.

3. A busker playing her guitar in an underground station; a hat on the ground contains a few coins which passers-by have thrown in.

4. A table at a wedding reception in a Western European country; the six guests are standing and toasting the bride and groom.

5. A small group of women in an aerobics class; they have clearly worked up a sweat as their shoulders glisten in the sunlight pouring in through the windows.

6. A father reprimanding his teenage daughter, who is sitting on her bed looking defiant.

You can read a commentary on this task on page 97.

If the materials you are producing are for use in your own classroom or within a school or area that you know very well, it's possible that some of the restrictions noted in the commentary for this task will not apply. Use your best judgement based on what you know about your specific 'market'.

Time-saving tips
For speaking tasks based on photographs, it's usually a good idea to find the image or images – or at least, a selection of possible images – that could be used, before you write the task. This is particularly important when writing for a publisher: you may ask the picture editor to find a photograph of a monkey doing juggling tricks on a monocycle, but perhaps such a photo does not exist. Finding the photo or photos yourself could save time in the long run.

DISCUSSION QUESTIONS

Different examinations have different formats for discussion. If you are required to write a number of questions on a particular topic, it is usual for these to be asked in ascending order of difficulty, to move from the personal to the more general, the concrete to the more abstract.

Task 11

The following questions on schools and education might be asked at a B2 level. Rank them from 1–6, assigning 1 to the question to be asked first, and 6 to the question to be asked last.

What might be the advantages of schools having shorter summer holidays?

How well do you think schools prepare young people for the world of work?

What are the qualities of a good teacher?

If you could afford it, would you send your child to a private school? Why (not)?

Should teachers be allowed to impose strict punishments on pupils who break school rules? Why (not)?

What are/were your least favourite subjects at school? Why?

You can read a commentary on this task on page 98.

Commentaries On Tasks

Task 2

Multiple-choice cloze, possible distractors:
1 A well   **B far**   C soon   D long
2 A Despite   B While   C Whereas   **D However**
or
A Besides   B Therefore   C Otherwise   **D However**
3 A wanted   B told   **C decided**   D discussed
4 **A turned**   B came   C resulted   D ended
5 **A raise**   B lift   C grow   D increase
6 A arrive   B reach   C appear   **D come**
7 A put   **B take**   C make   D give
or
A use   **B take**   C occupy   D claim
8 A worked   B earned   **C paid**   D gained
9 **A great**   B wide   C long   D excessive
10 A uniquely   B apart   C separately   **D alone**

Notes

2 *Although* might be considered by some to be correct here, so I have avoided using it as a distractor.

9 Did you consider using words such as *large*, *grand* and *high* for number 9? They may not often be used with *enthusiasm* but it seems, from online examples, that they might be possible and therefore, perhaps, better to avoid. *Wide* means *widespread* in this context so it can be used as a distractor here; *excessive* is ruled out by the following sentence; *long* does not collocate.

10 I have included two pairs of words here; *apart/alone* and *uniquely/separately*. See my comments on what to bear in mind when writing distractors.

How To Write Exam Preparation Materials

Task 3

Open cloze, possible gaps:

Dining alone
The growing trend in UK restaurants (0) <u>NOT</u> to accept reservations has a fortunate side-effect for the lone diner. A no-reservations policy can lead (1) <u>to</u> queues forming outside the more popular restaurants as diners wait (2) <u>for</u> a table to become available.

or

A no-reservations policy can **result** (1) <u>in</u> queues forming outside the more popular restaurants as diners wait for a table (2) <u>to</u> become available.

Understandably, perhaps, some are far from happy about having to stand outside a doorway (3) <u>before</u> settling down to a relaxing meal. People in parties of four or more often have a long wait. (4) <u>However</u>, those who choose or are forced to dine alone usually have (5) <u>no</u> trouble **at all** getting a table and are seated almost immediately.

This is obviously good news for solo diners, (6) <u>who</u> now make up a significant percentage of the restaurant-going public in the UK. 'A table for one, please' is now a common request to waiters, and people sitting (7) <u>on</u> their own are no longer made to feel as if they are rather odd. They can hold up their head with confidence (8) <u>instead</u> of trying to avoid unwelcome stares from fellow diners.

Comments

1 Students need to understand that *queues forming* is a result of a *no-reservations policy* and then, of course, identify the correct preposition.

2 You might gap the word *to* after *table* instead, though that would mean the answers to 1 and 2 would both be *to*. To avoid this, you could change the verb *lead* to *result* so that the key to 1 is *in*.

3 The order of events – *standing outside (in a queue)* then *settling down to a relaxing meal* – means that *before* is the only possible answer if it is gapped. Other possibilities might be either of the two words in *far from* at the beginning of the sentence. Gapping *far* would be more challenging.

4 Students need to recognise the contrast between *people in parties ... have a long wait* and *those who ... dine alone ... are seated almost immediately*.

5 The text says that lone diners *are seated almost immediately*, which will indicate to students that a negative word rather than a positive one (e.g. *some*, *great*) is required here. Adding the words *at all* reinforces *no* as the key and rules out *little* as a possible answer.

6 Weak students might be tempted to write *they*, *that* or even *which* (if they mistake *diners* for *dinners*). *This* at the beginning is another possibility, though you would probably need to accept *That* as an alternative key, even though it is slightly less natural here. The phrasal verb *make up* is a further possible target, though this might be considered too difficult for B2 students.

7 *On* is an obvious choice, but if you feel that enough prepositions are already in the key, you could gap either *their* or, for more challenge, *own* – there is enough context before and after the gap to support this.

8 As with 5, students need to recognise the contrast, this time within the same sentence, and of course, choose the right word.

Task 4

Listening: comments

Choice of topic
A *steam tractor rally* is rather culture-bound and many learners of English will have little or no schematic knowledge of this. This might well be an obstacle to their making sense of what is being said.

Language used
The language is very unnatural and would sound odd when recorded. One assumes this is intended to be an informal conversation, yet there are no contractions. There is also a mix of registers (*really cool* vs *most of them were constructed in the first quarter of the last century*) and expressions such as *not one to go in for that sort of thing* and *it is really up my street* would be lost on a B1 learner. This in itself is not a problem – students need to learn to deal with unknown language – but these two come in quick succession and also may, for all the student knows, have some bearing on the answer.

Options A–C
The answer is clearly option A, but knowing this relies on students understanding one item of vocabulary, *worn out*, which is probably unknown to most B1 learners of English. More support is needed in the script.

Option B is not about what Paul thought of the tractor rally (*it* in options A and C) – it describes his mother's reaction and therefore doesn't answer the question. Apart from that, the piece of dialogue which is relevant to this incorrect option, or distractor, (*I do not think my mother would have enjoyed it*, etc.) is along the right lines, but the sudden mention of his mother is forced here and very unnatural.

There is no really obvious language in the script to tempt students to choose **option C**. This is certainly not a prerequisite for a distractor – the fact that it is a plausible option is often enough – though it would not be difficult to include something here (e.g. *a friend of mine went and told me it wasn't very good, but I never listen to him anyway*).

Length
The length of the dialogue – just over 100 words – is good for a multiple-choice question at this and all levels. The recording will last around 30–40 seconds. Any shorter and it is difficult to work in the language which might tempt students to choose one of the distractors; much longer and it might become rambling and irrelevant.

TASK 5

Listening: Sentence completion

The wording of the sentences in questions 1–4 in Version A paraphrases the wording in the script, and as such, offers more challenge than Version B, where the sentences use exactly the same words as the script. For question 2 for example, the wording of the script in both versions is *we've decided to hire a coach for the journey*: this is paraphrased for the question in Version A as *The scouts are going to travel by coach to Portugal*, whereas in Version B, the wording is reproduced as *The organisers have decided to hire a coach for the journey to Portugal.* Version B is rather too easy in this respect.

Distraction is included in Version A, for questions 2 and 3, but not in Version B; in Version A two other forms of transport are mentioned in the script as distractors for question 2, and two other amounts of money appear as distractors for question 3. Once again, Version B offers less challenge as a result, particularly if students are allowed to hear the recording twice. (If they only hear it once, then this might be a more acceptable level of challenge.)

The spacing between each answer in the script for Version B is much shorter than in Version A. Students would have problems answering question 3 in Version B as this comes rather too quickly after the answer for question 2. Students need time to write each answer and then to recover and prepare themselves for the next one.

The answer to question 1 in both versions is *log cabins*: this is probably asking too much of level B1/B2 students, for whom this would be an unknown item of vocabulary. It would probably be better to change the script and the key to *tents*. In addition, the sentence in question 1 of version B allows for multiple keys, that is, several answers are possible, some of which students would not know how to spell; i.e. *Aveiro, Portugal, Sao Jacinto, a nature reserve, the Sao Jacinto nature reserve*. The equivalent sentence in version A has been structured so as to rule out these possible keys.

Question 4 in version A is too difficult. The script has been written in such a way that the clue in the script, *Have a look at photos of it online*, which equates with the wording in the question, appears quite some time after the mention of the key, i.e. *the beach*. This is unfair and asking too much of students at this level. Even at higher levels this type of feature would cause problems. If you are writing for a specific national or international examination, you should check past papers to see if this type of thing occurs. If it does not, then be sure not to include it in your own writing.

TASK 6

Possible questions:
(These are the actual questions I wrote for this task. There will, of course, be other possibilities.)

Phillip
Text: ... the sensation is one of being on permanent holiday.
Question: I do not feel as if I am working.

Text: ... possessions; I do my best to keep them to the bare minimum.
Question: I try not to accumulate personal belongings.

Dougie
Text: I come from a long line of travelling showmen .... It's been in my family's blood or nearly two centuries.
Question: Many of my ancestors had the same kind of lifestyle.

Text: ... because conditions are a bit cramped, we get on each other's nerves quite a lot.
Question: The nature of my living space often leads to tensions.

Text: It's a tough life, but I don't see myself doing anything else – there's nothing else I'd rather do.
Question: I could not imagine having a different lifestyle.

TASK 7

Possible options:
The correct answer is underlined. (These are the actual options I wrote for this task. There will, of course, be other possibilities.)

3 What do we learn about Jenny's clients?
A They cannot afford to buy the surveillance equipment.
B They object to paying such high prices for the work.
C <u>They do not want to do the detective work themselves.</u>
D They prefer more than one detective to work on a case.

Distractors A and B pick up on information in the text relating to cost. Distractor D is loosely based on the last sentence; *Finding out the truth is often just too painful to do on your own.*

4 How does Jenny feel about telling her story in the last paragraph?
A <u>embarrassed</u>
B frightened
C proud
D angry

Notice how Jenny's feeling is not overtly stated in the text, but it is clear from her physical reaction as stated in the second sentence of this paragraph, that she is embarrassed about how she came to be a private detective. An understanding of *She gives a slight grin* is necessary to rule out D (angry); C (proud) is less tempting, though the word *confides* might be confused with the meaning of *confident*; there is no indication that she is frightened (B).

Task 8

1. The question requires students to describe places and make recommendations in an informal letter, and is therefore probably intended for students with a B1 or B2 level. The question assumes that students are familiar with at least two different places by the sea. And if they live in a landlocked country, the assumption is that they have travelled abroad. Younger students might have little or no travel experience

2. This question assumes a knowledge of how technology is used, for example, to enhance sporting performance and improve refereeing decisions. It also assumes the student has the lexical resources to describe this technology and the ability to use sporting vocabulary, probably at B2 and above.

3. The question assumes that there is public transport where the students live, which may not be the case if their home is in a remote area. It should not, of course, be too difficult to invent a scenario for the sake of their answer, but this might put them at a disadvantage compared to other students.

4. The level of language in the question (*hand in one's notice, breathe a sigh of relief*) assumes a more advanced level, around C1 or above. Story writing tends to be associated with exams at B1 or B2 level, but students at this level would probably not understand the sentence.

5. The obvious assumption is that the students have experience — either now or in the past — of working in a management role. They will, we can safely assume, also be adults. They would probably also need to be at, or above, a B2 level, in order to be able to use the appropriate work-related language.

Task 9

1. Here is part of an email you receive from your English friend. Write a reply to your friend.
We aren't sure where to go for our beach holiday this year and we need some help to decide. Can you recommend a couple of decent places you know? What do you think we'd like about them?

Ideas
Depends on experience. Could choose one popular resort and another quieter holiday destination.

Language
Describing places
e.g. *(popular) seaside resort, (quiet) coastal town/village, (stroll along the) promenade, (lovely) sandy beach, (pleasant) holiday destination*

Describing the benefits
e.g. *soft sand, crystal-clear water, gentle waves, spotlessly clean, peace and quiet, lively and bustling, not too crowded, offers a wide range of possibilities, a variety of entertainment*

Making recommendations
e.g. *You might like to try/prefer, It is worth considering, Another interesting place is, A good spot for (watersports, sunbathing) is, Its main advantage is*

Structures
Possibly language of comparatives to compare the two recommendations.

2. Write an essay on the following question: *Is the use of technology in sport a good or a bad thing?*

Ideas

<u>A good thing</u>
Improves performance (e.g. clothing for athletes, rackets for tennis players)
Helps refereeing decisions (e.g. tennis, football) – makes sport fairer.
Improves safety (e.g. design of protective clothing/helmets)

<u>A bad thing</u>
Dominates sport – technological performance not human performance
Makes sport dull and mechanical – takes away the excitement of human error in refereeing decisions
Not everyone can afford the technology
Encourages cheating in sport (e.g. performance-enhancing drugs)

Language

<u>Relevant sport vocabulary</u> (see also Ideas section above)
E.g. *score a goal, hit a tennis ball hard/over the net, win a point, referee, linesman, umpire, goal-line technology, full-length swimsuit, headgear, footwear, clothing*

<u>Collocations</u>
improve performance/enjoyment, heighten interest, diminish the enjoyment, reduce the human element, give/gain an (unfair) advantage, maximize safety, have a beneficial/harmful/positive/negative effect (on), bend the rules

3. Write a report for the local council on public transport services where you live. Describe what services are available and suggest ways in which they can be improved.

Ideas
Depends on services.
Suggestions for improvements could include:

- increasing frequency of services
- increasing number of routes
- improving comfort on buses, trains, etc.
- facilities for the disabled (e.g. wheelchair areas on trains, lifts in underground)
- better parking facilities at train stations

Language

Describing transport services

e.g. *(in)frequent, (un)reliable, (un)comfortable, (the village) has good/poor transport links with (other towns), (the town) is (not) well served by public transport*

Making suggestions

e.g. *I recommend that the council should (improve), I suggest (increasing), There is a great need for (parking facilities), (Wheelchair areas) should be introduced (on trains)*

4. Write a story beginning with the following sentence: *She handed in her notice and breathed a sigh of relief.*

Ideas

Limitless possibilities. Could either tell story leading up to this moment, or describe what happened afterwards, or both.

Language

This depends on the story. However, one would expect a variety of past tenses, appropriate cohesive devices and a range of language at the same level as the two collocations in the opening sentence.

5. Your company's in-house magazine is running a series of articles on jobs in management within the company. You have been asked to write an article on your own management position, explaining your role, describing the challenges of the job and the qualities required to meet those challenges.

Ideas
The content clearly depends on the management position described and the nature of the company. However, the structure of the article is clear: explain your role, describe the challenges, describe the qualities required.

Language
Explaining your role
e.g. *My duties include, The main part of my job/The bulk of my work involves (+ gerund), The position consists in (+ gerund), The job requires me* (+ full infinitive)

Describing the challenges of the job
e.g. *The hardest challenge I face is (trying to solve), One of the most difficult aspects is (the pressure I face from),* [plus the language in 'Explaining your role' above]

Describing the qualities required
e.g. *an attention to detail, an enthusiastic approach to work, strong leadership qualities, good interpersonal skills, an outgoing/easy-going/patient, etc. nature, a willingness to adapt, an ability to listen, etc.*

Task 10

1. It is unlikely that this photo will have model release, that is, permission from every single person — or in this case, the parents of the children — in the photograph for the photo to be used in published material which will be sold for commercial gain.

2. For religious and/or cultural reasons, some markets will not use a book containing references to, or photographs of pigs.

3. There are no apparent reasons why this photograph cannot be used.

4. It is very likely that there will be alcohol in the glasses being used to toast the bride and groom. This would not be acceptable for some markets.

5. The glistening shoulders suggest that rather too much of the female body is exposed in this photograph for some markets. In this case, it would be wise to aim for photos where as much of the body is covered up as possible.

6. Unfortunately, a seemingly innocent photo of a man alone in a bedroom with a teenage girl may be interpreted in a completely different way to that which is intended.

TASK 11

There is clearly no answer to this task. Here is the order I would ask them in, with my reasons for doing so.

Students will be able to comment on these from experience.
1 What are/were your least favourite subjects at school? Why?
2 What are the qualities of a good teacher?

Students have experience of both holidays and discipline; they are asked to hypothesize on aspects of these topics which they may have considered.
3 What might be the advantages of schools having shorter summer holidays?
4 Should teachers be allowed to impose strict punishments on pupils who break school rules? Why (not)?

This question opens the topic out to a more general area.
5 How well do you think schools prepare young people for the world of work?

Students hypothesize on a topic they may not have considered before.
6 If you could afford it, would you send your child to a private school? Why (not)?

Glossary

affixation
Affixation is the process of adding material to a word to create a different form of that word (e.g. *tree → trees*), a word which is a different part of speech (e.g. *sad → sad**ness***) or a word with a different meaning (*happy → **un**happy*). The parts shown in bold in the examples are known as *affixes*. Affixes which are added to the end of the base word (e.g. ***-ness***) are called suffixes; those added to the beginning of the base word (e.g. ***un-***) are called prefixes.

coherence
The ability of a text or piece of dialogue to make sense is called coherence. Language which is coherent is clear, well organised and easy to understand. All the ideas and arguments connect or follow in a natural and logical way. Compare the following:
Coherent: Roger Bannister was the first man to run a mile in under four minutes. This historic event took place in Oxford on May 6th 1954.
Incoherent: Roger Bannister was the first man to run a mile in under four minutes. This is not the kind of thing you'd expect her to do so early in the day.

cohesion
Cohesion refers to the grammatical and lexical linking that joins together the different parts of a text to give it meaning. Cohesion can be achieved by using devices such as conjunctions (e.g. *but, although, so*), discourse markers (e.g. *as a result, in addition, however, fortunately*), demonstrative adjectives (*this, that, these, those*) and reference pronouns (e.g. *he, him, this, one*).

Note: In the 'incoherent' Roger Bannister example for **coherence** above, there is apparent *cohesion* (the demonstrative pronoun *This* in the second sentence seems at first to refer back to the event in the first sentence) but the lack of *coherence* makes the sentence incomprehensible.

collocation
A collocation is a pair or group of words that commonly occur together e.g. *bitterly disappointed, a wide range of goods, provide an insight into*.

distractor
Distractors are the incorrect options in a multiple-choice question.

distraction
Distraction, here, is used to refer to language included in a reading text or listening script which might cause students to write or choose an incorrect answer.

gist
The gist is the general idea or meaning conveyed by the writer in a reading text or a speaker in a listening script.

lexical
Lexical is the adjective from *lexis* and relates to vocabulary.

lexico-grammatical
Lexico-grammatical describes areas of language which involve considerations of both lexis and grammar. The lexical phrase *a great deal of* is followed by an uncountable noun such as *money*, whereas *a large number of* is followed by a plural countable noun such as *coins*. Similarly, *cause* and *result* are two items of lexis with a similar meaning but different grammar: *cause* is a transitive verb followed by a

direct object (*The earthquake caused widespread destruction*); *result* is followed by the preposition *in* (*The earthquake resulted in widespread destruction*).

multiple-choice cloze test
A gap-filling task in which words have been removed from a text. Students are given a number of options for each gap and they have to decide which of these options best fits the gaps.

multiple keys
If a question has multiple keys, it means a number of different answers are possible. In the following sentence, for example, the words *While, Whilst, Whereas, Although, Though* can all be used to complete the gap:
_____ *some novelists become very wealthy, most struggle to make a decent living.*

open cloze test
A gap-filling task in which words have been removed from a text. Unlike the **multiple-choice cloze test**, students are given no options to choose from and have to come up with the answers themselves.

paraphrase (n/v)
If you paraphrase what someone has written or said, you express the same meaning using different words. E.g. *She probably won't come* is a paraphrase of *She's unlikely to come.*

schematic knowledge
Schematic knowledge refers to what we know about the world and the way it works. For example, if we know and can visualise what happens in a football match – if we have a well-developed schema for football – we will be able to make sense of the following statement: *He was substituted after he got the yellow card; they couldn't afford to lose*

him for the next match. If we don't have that particular schematic knowledge, (if we don't know that players can be substituted during a match, what yellow cards are, or that two yellow cards mean a player is sent off and automatically misses the next match) we might struggle to understand the sentence.

Titles in this series are ...

A Lexicon For ELT Professionals
How ELT Publishing Works
How To Plan A Book
How To Write And Deliver Talks
How To Write Audio and Video Scripts ↗
How To Write Business English Materials †
How To Write CLIL Materials
How To Write Corporate Training Materials †
How To Write Critical Thinking Activities ↗
How To Write EAP Materials †
How To Write ESOL Materials †
How To Write ESP Materials †
How To Write Exam Preparation Materials
How To Write Film And Video Activities
How To Write For Digital Media
How To Write Graded Readers
How To Write Grammar Presentations And Practice
How To Write Inclusive Materials
How To Write Primary Materials
How To Write Pronunciation Activities
How To Write Reading And Listening Activities ↗
How To Write Secondary Materials
How To Write Speaking Activities ↗
How To Write Teacher's Books
How To Write Vocabulary Presentations And Practice ↗
How To Write Worksheets
How To Write Writing Activities ↗

Our paperback compendiums

↗ *How To Write Excellent ELT Materials: The Skills Series*
This book contains the six titles marked ↗ above.

† *How To Write Excellent ELT Materials: The ESP Series*
This book contains the five titles marked † above.

For further information, see **eltteacher2writer.co.uk**

Printed in Great Britain
by Amazon